Velvet Grapes

drunk midnight poetry

SNEHA BHURA

Hawakal
PUBLISHERS
Calcutta | New Delhi

hawakal

CALCUTTA | NEW DELHI

Hawakal Publishers

70-B/9 Amritpuri, East of Kailash, New Delhi 65
33/1/2 K B Sarani, Mall Road, Calcutta 80

Email info@hawakal.com
Website www.hawakal.com

Cover art by Shutterstock

Cover designed by Bitan Chakraborty

First edition: January 2021

ISBN: 978-81-950350-2-1

Price: INR 250 | USD 10.99

Our object-choices

DRUNK MIDNIGHT POETRY

In a near-empty park
with the last of the winter sun
in full flush
I finally laughed
delirious with a date
after a string of lousy dates
a cackling that mocked
more than a year's sorrow
over a debilitating heartbreak.
And then, just as suddenly,
the world paused.

When Delhi imposed a lockdown on 23 March, before any other city in India, the heart feared the worst again.

There was an image of him waiting for me at the park that kept spinning inside my head long after we were all shuttered home. An image of him going round and round in circles, with his face lowered and sweetly scrunched up. Every night, in a large living room bathed in soft yellow light, I would laugh and cry—giddily swing between joy and despair to the sound of the most breathtaking music. In my frenzied state, I would go over the minutiae of that wondrous evening like my only salvation. One particularly agonizing night, I instinctively reached out for a pen and notepad. I knew I had to rid myself of that unrelenting image. I had to pin down this heart-sickening fiend on paper to see it for what it was. I tried writing a short story around this stubborn image but felt that was too laborious and contrived. When I realized I needed relief that was quicker and leaner, I began writing short, staccato lines. It flowed out more organically to the sound of music. I found poetry in a pandemic. In all these years I never quite understood or appreciated the sheer sheltering silence that poetry offers. It took a pandemic-induced lockdown—combined with my own desperate bid to save one hope-instilling event from melting into inconsequence—to heave out my fear and anguish into midnight poems. Since then there's been no looking back.

For over eight months since April, I followed and plumbed words brewing out of a torpid emotional state. Found myself drifting and dreaming with songs that rhymed with my thoughts and fueled words onto the page. Slowly and imperceptibly, the nightly ritual became a zone of resilience, a place where I could float above the uncertainty around me, ride out a strange matrix of loneliness, fear, and anxiety. The few hours in the night when I have poetry and music, the past and the future they cease to oppress. I feel a great sense of control—I flourish in a keenly felt playpen of my own. Thankfully, the date I found in March was like deciphering a code, an elusive charmer with seemingly little to lose. I learned to be unperturbed, to wait, surrender, and let go—with an aching realization that I don't control outcomes.

It is poetry combined with music that has shown me what self-containment might be like; it has taught me how to practice detachment in a crisis. So what follows in a miscellany of light lockdown poems on dates, flatmates and phoney friends produced with all the extraordinary angst befitting this period in history. They also come with a specially curated playlist to act as a breather while dipping into its bright, buttery waters.

But this kind of a drunk,
unruly fetishization of a date
is as tart and obscure
as a velvet grape.

Sneha Bhura
December 2020
New Delhi

ACKNOWLEDGMENTS

Thank you Anindita, my poetry paramour, for being endlessly patient and poised.

Dinsa, who should be a hipster shrink for working millenials.

Ruchika, combat yogini, who is all 'energy' and 'secret messenger.'

Rahul, always there, idiotic and unperturbed.

Andy, the dating don from Dubai.

CONTENTS

Spring-on-Pause

I saw you standing in the park,
waiting, wondering, eager and unquiet
awkward and faraway
you kept whirling a circle,
staring at your feet.

You gazed not into my eyes,
rambling, jesting, singing and snarky.
Curly-cute and deadpan-cool —
my heart hummed a moonly tune
from a magic midsummer night.

Glee soared to the sky
laughter spilled sideways
teasing, searching, bright and green
walking now, side-sitting then
a day so brilliantly kind,
at long last, I wished it didn't end.

But now I think of you,
in slow, lingering sadness
locked, hunkered, sealed and shut-in,
star-crossed stuck and heart's-a-limbo.
When bastard bats swooped out of a cave,
the gravediggers surrendered in despair.

How I feel dead and alive in seclusion
slippery, illusive, lost and dazed.
Computer love, fleet-foot smoothie,
distance is the shape of this great affliction.
Loony little spook,
you'll still be uttered as benediction.

Your deep drunk radio voice
is a monkey on my back.
Rolling, frisky, gurgling and breezy.
Backwards walker, elfin talker,
I am secretly coasting on a pause—
clutching on a frenzy, once in deep frost.

A Memory Stick in Adriatic Blue

A miracle pen-drive
fell into my palm;
blue and silver, sleek and small.
A yankee doodle darling,
quaint and calm, set it sail
after a drunken midnight brawl.

Quivering in its shell,
delicate and cold
it flashed a thousand fiery rays
like a fountain aflame.
Dewdrop in Adriatic blue, sweeter than gold,
you had me hopping, leaping lame.

Trophy thumbelina,
snug in the pistil of my hand
no dank data could be your host
nor a mote of dust in your beam ever did land.
Idle and unspoiled,
I could only stare, flaunt and boast.

But fragile, beautiful seldom,
you were a wretched curse.
How you drove out from the get-go!
When you slyly ran off with the hearse,
I never thought of your kind
without grief or woe.

7'o Clock Somewhere

Fridays, next to Moulin Rouge,
a winking karaoke bar
with cut-price booze
had us scurry like squirrels after seven.
One could smoke inside
under the sputtering lights
in our rinky-dink piece of heaven.

Always, a repetitive motion disorder,
gin soda cheeseballs, I ordered.
Golden corny disco balls stuffed my gut
for you, half an eye-roll,
beer and mushroom stuffed.
The waiter with midnight eyes
forever obliged; barely a tut-tut.

Upstairs, we hawk-eyed
that cosy little nook
where grubby glass walls
oversaw the babbling brook

of would-be Don Juans
and humming maidens
wayward roadsigns
and mangy transformer dolls.
But how we knew,
only the mother-jockey had the balls.

Cigarettes, we flicked on with mint.
What's with the switch,
you'd sometimes hint.
I rambled, whooped and wailed,
more than I inhaled.
There was no home or hurry to care
where could I repair, if not there?

Jolene, the song
swirled in the sooty air,
in the lacerated sofa,
in our wind-tossed hair.
Singing drunk on a mike,
we never truly liked.
In this muck of a night dive
we chorused each other
aglow and alive.

Bunker Blues

Morning, noon, evening, night
is summer, spring, autumn, winter
is breakfast, lunch, apple, dinner
is work, stream, cook, dither
is you, flatmate, grocer, mother.
This is the architecture and dejecture
of my spectral days
of leaning lamps with stilted rays.

Newspaper, office, snacking, reading
is dreaming, wondering, starving, staring
is PDF, omelettes, careening, carousing
is longing, stalking, withholding, waiting
is you, landlord, rice and biscuit Nice.
This is the circadian groove
and leaping loop of my swivel-eyed cycle
on a Naugahyde couch with music vital

Cooking-of-Age

My dinner is calm and easy.
The brown slab of striped rectangle
with lighted green reds and yellows
is pillar, post and greasy.

Tomatoes, onion and chilies
get diced in no predestined way.
I wait for eddies of songs
to ordain the last hunky course of the day.

Orange lentils stuffed in muslin
jigger and sway like bundled dumplings,
amidst rice and potatoes, in a coppery cooker—
slack-hack remedy from the spiffy mother.

Stray unwashed utensils dawdle in the sink
stubborn everyday detritus of the flatmate;
she urgently needs a shrink,
though if I tell her so, she could bite or wince.

In this stilled kitchen cauldron
scrubbing, scouring, rinsing, draining
I tilt and bend and arc and gaze
like Chardin's cellar boy and the scullery maid.

But help now I do not thee seek.
for I, the lady of the cookhouse,
dreamy, disheveled, frying-pan louse
has found sustenance and sleep.

Airtight Chase

They like it fizzy and sparkling,
like soda pop
eno shock, and
highball rocks.

Fruit punch and iced tea
you should not be.
A half-caffeinated disposition
is lovely, dark and deep.

When gin-soaked maudlin,
coolness will creep in.
Vodka volatile
is strictly ill advised.

But gone you are,
a wretched drunk in the dumps.
For there ain't no hunk
who loves a good funk.

Earthquake Kit

A tiny essence of damask rose
for jangled nerves to compose.
A flask of Tequila grapefruit
to chug after breathless scoot.

Lip balm in papaya and peach
always buried beyond reach.
Now with a black silk eye patch
rests front-center of the bag.

A tessellated volume of Rumi
for shuddering hours so gloomy.
Bluebird box of silvery bangles
was a desperate, last minute wrangle.

Waterproof kohl for a Cleopatra eye
to cry, sniffle and sigh.
And those overpriced Ray-bans
when earth scuttles best laid plans.

This is in anticipation
of a Capital devastation.
Even as we quake in our boots
of a virus which gives no hoots!

Once Upon a Fire

A flaming dark tree
outside my window
sparkles and singes
an amoebic ball of fire
spreading a scene so dire
tangled up electric wires
this is excitement in limbo.

A grizzly bear uncle
with naked arms
woofs and barks
rides his zippy vespa
like a man-in-charge.
He is dragon, he is hell fire
raging ballsy grocer
you need not hire

Yet another tree inflames
on a sizzling summer night
dry rasping leaves

in electric blue light.
There is no panic or fright
we are bored, trapped and tired
attuned to everyday exploding fires.
So out it goes itself;
tonight there are no buyers.

Transmission

I was talking to you
in my head
telling you a sad story
I wanted to be
choking deep watery
so you believed
I wasn't just
a wild, cackling heap!
I dredged up my father
from the caverns,
that long frigid spell
I gathered.
And told you,
about the time
we didn't speak at all.
But as I began
to lay the land,
it suddenly dawned
glowed and wailed,
a gasping pool

of quicksand.
There he was
choking and gutted,
unable to get
the blistering secret
of my heart;
we were both
so grievously ripped apart
stunned
into a cold, crippling disregard.
There was nothing I could do
neither did he try, too.
How I broke
into consolable, soothing sobs
I called him the next day—
to talk of hospital beds
and vanishing jobs.

En-cryptic

You have a desk with a view
of skies sweeping white
and cerulean blue.
I squint and lean over,
peer down from your window—
a splay of tiny brown dots
and fractional green stocks.
Quietly, from my W chatbox.

A distant tree in the frame
is the back of your lovely lost head
lost in the drifting white
sparse, like your clean brown desk.
The rolling tip of your notepad
is a hint and a code; it makes me mad!
As elusive in the view
as in my bright green W.

Righteous Bully

Something devious
when you squinch your eyes,
and crinkle your face, like
'Do you not see the obvious,'
 you want to say.

Something rotten
in your self-indulgent spread
of salad purple flaccid
and cold, untoasted bread.
'This is how you host, bed-head!'

Sour-tongued seniority
is your badge and your watermark.
About bygone bitches, you always bark.
Pray, why wear me out so
even while smoking up?

Red Room Raving

Autoplay in crisis
no money can fix it
once, fostered unbidden
an extradimensional playlist
in a sultry red room
which flared and burned
on 27 June.

You showed me red
which like an idiot
I did not ever see.
Did not even see
those impish eyes—
we sealed in a nebulous space
from 2 lakh cases in 12 days.

Pizza and polaroids,
hung curd and goblet gin
on a night so muggy
all desired your company.

Slow heat surged and prickled
before and after the deed.
28 June midnight,
you left me a stick of weed.

A sudden, savage balcony kiss
I now search and sorely miss.
Whispers in soft, smoky drawls
cooed in my ears, as I rolled
drunk in your thrall.
When Autoplay was back
21 July was wistful, wracked,
aching for yet another crack.

Boy With a Helmet

Motorcycle heartbreaker
you sped off
like a rubik's toy boy
in green and blue checks
the world teeming
with all your ex-es.

You played the uke
rolled a great many joints
I lent you some books
you made off with polaroids
sweet and intent in playful pink,
how you wink and shrink.

Your teatime butt slaps
left a heavy brain fog
vapours of your cigarettes
linger and tarry
in piquant vignettes
Fucker slept like a log!

But tender was the night
when you held forth
in long, looping lines
you flipped the painting right.
A big, fruity emerald ring,
grubby fingers all ting-a-ling.

Age of Anxiety

Sunday savior
waiting gets crazier
two rapturous weekends
eager and ravenous
what came after?
Placative promises
and hints ominous.

I cancel all plans
make no weekend one
rascal hope; f***face rogue
a dream of a face
how you shun and run
for a "kibbutz" with friends!
Is this dissipation? Are you done?

Under lights midnight yellow
I feel your presence
with poems placid and songs mellow
howling for the North Country Fair,

with splendid, unkempt hair.
That shy lean into a halfway tune
my bad, my man, my moon.

Flatmate

Chilled out you are not.
Though you bake a lot,
sweet and scrumptious?
Not by a long shot!

Teased out I haven't
neither a twinkle or a beam
in this vast, confining dream,
you are stiff-necked supreme.

Kind you are only when I cry,
else you shut yourself in
hiding, biding, never colliding,
while I stew, simmer and fry.

Sledgehammered you have,
my food, friends and fellas
with looks lordly and callow gab.
Housing with you is deadly drab.

Covidating

Dark-haired night owl,
how you make me howl!
Another courting app calamity
quelled and crushed to insanity.

I stubbornly cling,
to a coolly flippant fling
who types Lol and Lel
it doesn't feel so swell.

On long, fallow days
you have your invisible ways.
When suddenly a text leaps out,
I jump, twist and shout.

Long stuck in a crevasse
verses bleed with a menace.
You make me a lovesick puppy
fevered nightly on songs so sappy.

So I pray and cry and wait
for a pandemic to abate
with a sad, fearful heart.
It's then back to the start.

Dispiration

On some vacant nights
love and its demons
skive and snooze
silken waves of music
simmer down, vamoose.
Hands ball into a fist,
rummaging thoughts,
ideas, an object to enlist.

The lights don't pulse;
on a big black couch
I flail and convulse.

It's time
to breathe and brood
to float and sing
be hip and drowsy
splayed out, in-housey.

Magic Laconic

Always at the back
I itch and ache
to see your face
dreaming and displaced.

You are a vanishing
brief, flinty, evanescing
a lightning bug,
sandbox and a slug.

Pink Vodka

Two buttcracking hearts
on a resolute hip flask
is an ounce of coupling.

Drink and you miss
a rouse and fall hiss
of bubble berry white
and orange liquid.

A tail-end chug
from a big-bowl jug—
and a round of tittering.

Drinking with you
on a moonless night
is rich and puckering.

Ukulele

First in checks
then a boat-neck
with oblong glasses
then wide-eyed without
a sun-dappled afternoon
'ere a rain-washed night
once bored and broody
then keen and kooky
you were video-shy
then camera-calm
distant and done
to peaches and plum
once ready to leave
later you stayed
and played
my dirty, white uke.
How will I recoup?

Boulder in a Park

Like a coconut tree climber,
you propel with a reptilian grace.
A slight, stumbling jerk
like holding by the waist
in a soft, cool embrace.
Coffee cup close to your face,
is a morning ritual I can't efface
acted on a garden-white table—
one absent newspaper
unfurling over a green gable.

Night after Night

Surreptitiously
Smilingly
Hesitatingly
Heart-stoppingly
Apprehensively
Agonizingly
Raveningly
Resignedly
Dying-ly
Doe-eyed-ly

I check if you're awake
pray you not be a rake.
A deep, nocturnal urge
heaves over and over,
in full surge.

The Song You Gave Me

On days I just can't say hi,
pensive on my couch I lie.
I dig up the Dylan you sang
its first few notes, startling,
a soft soar of a pang.

I picture you buttoned up
in a long light shirt, hunched
earnestly over your guitar.
Sophomore-sincere, boyish heart,
bespectacled dork, off-key lark.

A song you so easily deny
is my one brief respite
when you wither away, I try
when you slither away, I cry
6 months in, I still know not why.

Good Things

You are a good thing
you make me laugh
it's an upward graph
it only gets better
no go-getter
I write secret letters
you always expect better
there's no push greater
than a sparky, smug dater
who is music and poetry
knife-nosed smirky
you are always like later
absent, cryptic,
take take taker
still upwards
I, like a dumbwaiter.

Aunty

Covertly insecure,
you look unsure
with motives obscure
hobbling injury endure
and gift me a liqueur.

That shadow of a doubt
the goodly lines you spout
I really can do without
never a rule you flout
there's no depravity or drought?

Distrust I your natter yatter yap
trouble's with me perhaps.
Even so you praise and clap
all your domesticity crap.
How you no funniness lack?

What is There to Do

you can wait
for a casual "hey"
to make your day
you can write
your casual "hey"
in one thousand ways
but he will remain
a half-gone bird
bosky and blurred

Bathos

Stale cinnamon and
wilting rocket leaves
in the bitterest of eves
when jokes don't land.

Goa or pondicherry
need not disagree;
yet another smash
after badminton bland.

Checkered shirt, crumpled
brows, prickly and fraying
and thesis hypotheses
I do quite understand.

You suddenly fizzle out
and say goodnight.
Those neatly cut apples
I miss and be damned.

The Morning after

Muir notes
the sweatshirt spoke
big bear of a hug
the jumper called forth

you are no hugger
you take your rum
and head home
quick to sleep
quick to leave
how did I believe
the mad mush,
and the flutter?
Heart is in the gutter.

Signals

Frosted night
a hot bowl of soup
and The Crown 2+2.
Charles and Diana too
scrimmage in a soup.

To my surprise
later in the night
the one poem I behold
is Eros Turranos—
an unhappy marriage,
of keeping appearances.

I picture us
married, mismatched
despite appearances
unhappy the we
door rattles
couch trembles
it's true, o beaut!

The Letter

lack of graciousness,
ample overextension
is the crux and call
of a small exit note
bubbling over
foaming at the throat

lines in black san serif
swirl and surround
from discarded drafts
and deleted texts
friends call me unsound
if I call pining and vexed

sweet, shapely letters
of your name, it often looks
circular, sinister, strange
when I squint I know
you will always sail through
a moonshine missive
will not save you

PLAYLIST

Je pense à toi | Amadou & Mariam
Bongo Bong | Manu Chao
Sparring Partner | Paolo Conte
Piazza, New York Catcher | Belle & Sebastian
Lujon | Henry Mancini
Aht Uh Mi Hed | Shuggie Otis
Carmensita | Devendra Banhart
Baltimore | Nina Simone
Army Dreamers | Kate Bush
Comment te dire adieu | Françoise Hardy
Heartbeats | The Knife
Clown on the 22nd Floor | Peter Cat Recording Co.
Miss you | Carla Bruni
Say Goodbye | Norah Jones
Spooky | Dusty Springfield
Universal Traveler | Air
Booty Swing | Parov Stelar
Girl from the North Country | Bob Dylan
Dance with me | Nouvelle Vague, Mélanie Pain
En septembre sous le pluie | Léo Marjane
Andy Shauf | The Magician
Lying has to stop | Soft Hair, LA Priest, Connan Mockasin
All Tomorrow's Parties | The Velvet Underground, Nico
Heart of Glass | Blondie
Hunnybee | Unknown Mortal Orchestra
Ulysses and the Sea | Papooz
He Needs Me | Punch-Drunk Love
I am the Changer | Cotton Jones
My moon, my man | Feist
Doo Dah | Homeshake